# Stock Market Smart

Eileen Nixon McGowan
&
Nancy Lagow Dumas

**M**
THE MILLBROOK PRESS
BROOKFIELD, CONNECTICUT

# M

THE MILLBROOK PRESS

Design and Electronic Page Makeup by
JAFFE ENTERPRISES
Ron Jaffe

To Joan and Hershell Nixon, with love and gratitude. To Katie McGowan, my love forever and always. —ENM

To my daughter, Catherine Crawford Clements, and my granddaughter, Hannah Mae Clements. —NLD

Background cover image courtesy AP/ Wide World Photos, Inc.
Other images from the Hemera Technologies, Inc. Photo Objects collections

Published by
The Millbrook Press, Inc.
2 Old New Milford Road
Brookfield, Connecticut   06804

www.millbrookpress.com

Library of Congress Cataloging-in-Publication Data

McGowan, Eileen Nixon.
Stock market smart / by Eileen Nixon McGowan and Nancy Lagow Dumas.
    p. cm.
Includes index.
ISBN 0-7613-2113-6 (lib. bdg.)
1. Investments—Miscellanea—Juvenile literature. 2. Stocks—Miscellanea—Juvenile literature. I. Dumas, Nancy Lagow. II. Title.

HG4553 .M34 2002
332.63'22—dc21

                                                              2001032694


1  3  5  7  9  10  8  6  4  2

# Contents

| CHAPTER | PAGE |
|---|---|

# Introduction

Everyone thinks about money.

Our grandparents, our parents, our sisters and brothers, our friends—all of them talk about money: How do we earn it? Spend it? Invest it? Is there enough? Will there be enough in the future? Can we make our money grow? Can we afford what we want to buy? And, in just a few years, what about college expenses?

We think about saving money.

Sometimes our goals are small, short-term goals. Suppose we save to buy a book or a new CD. Our purchase won't cost much, so reaching our goal will take only a short time. A piggy bank could be a good place to keep our savings.

Sometimes our goals include needs or wishes that are larger. Maybe we want to buy a new bike or pay for two weeks at summer camp. It might take many months to earn and save the money we need. A savings account in a bank not only keeps our money safe but also pays interest, helping it grow.

Sometimes we have long-term goals. We look ahead to the future and save for college tuition or to study abroad. Maybe we dream of someday establishing a business of our own or owning a home. Putting our money to work in the stock market will help our savings grow faster and at a greater rate.

Piggy bank?

Savings account?

Bonds?

Stock market?

When it comes to investing, there are many questions that we need to think about. We know what money is, and we know that we need it to meet our expenses, but we must also understand our personal feelings about money.

Do we think of money as a reward?

Do we feel proud when we earn our own money?

Does money matter too much to us?

Or does it not matter enough?

Does the way we feel about money make a difference?

Yes, it does. As a financial consultant, I am well aware that we must understand our feelings in order to invest our money wisely.

In this book, we'll not only learn about the stock market—what it is, how it works, and what it can do for us—but we'll also examine the personal approach to investing that can bring us success.

*Nancy Lagow Dumas*

FINANCIAL ADVISER

CHAPTER 1

# The Stock Market: What Is It?

## What is a stock?

Sometimes a company wants to grow. Sometimes a company wants to research better ways of making its product or offering its services. Occasionally it wants to invent new products. In order to do these things, it needs money.

A company can raise money by selling shares in itself. This is called *issuing stock*. Stock represents ownership of a portion of a company. People, or **INVESTORS**, purchase it because they believe it will be successful. Companies issue many shares in themselves so that a lot of investors—hundreds, thousands, even millions—can own their stock.

## What is a stockholder?

You become a stockholder when you buy shares—or stock—in a company. When someone buys stock, he or she actually becomes one of the owners of that company. If the company does well financially, the person who bought the stock—the investor—will share in the **PROFITS**.

## How old must you be to buy stock?

You must be at least eighteen years of age. Until you reach that age your parents can invest for you in what is called a *custodial account*. You can be stock-market smart and let them know the

**WHAT'S THAT?**
An INVESTOR is a person like you and me who buys and sells stock, hoping it will bring a profit.

**WHAT'S THAT?**
PROFIT is the money earned beyond the amount of money invested and after taxes.

stocks you've studied carefully and want to buy. Later in this book, we'll show you how to study stocks and learn which would make good, well-thought-out investments for you.

## How much money do you need?

In order to open an account with a stockbroker you usually need to make an initial **INVESTMENT** of $1,000. However, you can find brokers on the Internet who require only $15 or $20 to open an account.

## How did the stock market begin?

Stock markets began in the 1600s. In England, people invested in the cargoes of ships, some of which were headed to the American colonies. If the ships arrived safely and their cargoes were sold to the colonists for a good price, the investors made a profit. It might have been a small profit or a very large profit, depending on how many shares the investors bought.

In the American colonies, people met at exchanges to invest in cargoes or crops going to Great Britain. For example, in Williamsburg, Virginia, in the 1700s, the exchange was held outdoors near a coffee shop close to the capitol.

The New York Stock Exchange traces its roots to 1792, when it did business under a buttonwood tree on a street called Wall Street. Here, twenty-four people, called brokers, signed an agreement that formed the first organized stock market in New York.

## How does the stock market work today?

At the New York Stock Exchange, for example, billions of dollars worth of stock are traded every business day. The trading floor may seem like loud chaos, but it is actually well organized.

**WHAT'S THAT?**
INVESTMENT means putting your money into something that offers the possibility of good returns or profit. An initial investment is your first investment.

7

WHAT'S THAT?
Stock trading is called TRADING because stock can't be bought unless someone wants to sell.

WHAT'S THAT?
A STOCK-BROKER, or broker, is a person certified and registered to buy and sell stock on behalf of investors. A broker tries to get the investor the best price.

Each day, except on weekends and holidays, the Exchange opens for **TRADING** at 9:30 A.M. Eastern Standard Time. At 4 P.M. the closing bell rings, ending trading for the day. For every buyer there is a seller, and their orders are matched up on the trading floor.

An investor calls a **STOCKBROKER** to purchase stock in a company. The stockbroker sends an order via phone or computer to the New York Stock Exchange. Around the edge of the Stock Exchange, in the broker booths, are member-firm brokers, each with a phone and a computer. A member-firm broker then gives the order, electronically or in written form, to a floor broker, who takes the order to the trading post on the floor of the Stock Exchange where that particular stock trades. Together, the floor broker and the specialist at the trading post, called a *market maker*, carry out the stock trade. They follow the client's order to buy or sell the stock. Through an auction process, they work to get the client the best price. The American Stock Exchange (AMEX) works in the same way. The National Association of Securities Dealers Automated Quotation (NASDAQ), however, is computerized.

Like a department store, which has one area for shoes, one for sportswear, another for costume jewelry, and so on, the Exchange has different areas where specific stocks are traded and information about those stocks is displayed. These are the trading posts, and they are located throughout the trading floor. They are staffed by specialists, who buy or sell stocks on order from the stockbroker, then report trades through computers. The transaction is complete. The sale is then reported back to the stockbroker and published on the ticker tape for anyone to see. The stockbroker places an **ELECTRONIC STOCK CERTIFICATE** in the client's file. The client sometimes receives a paper copy of the confirmation.

The stockbroker's company keeps a computer record of the stocks. When you and your parents choose to sell, the broker will sell the stock and send you a check, minus the broker's commission. Confirmation of the trade is done through the computer.

## Why doesn't an owner of a company just borrow the money he needs from a bank? Why does he want to sell shares in his company?

If businesses were to succeed in all their **VENTURES**, their owners could probably increase the size of their businesses or develop new products by borrowing money from banks, brokerages, insurance companies, or individual investors. But there are risks involved in any venture. By having more than one way of getting money for their ventures, businesses are able to spread out their risks.

Suppose that an automobile company develops a one-person car. The officers of the company think people will love one-person cars, so they spend a great deal of money making and advertising them. However, their research proves to be wrong. Most car buyers want larger automobiles, and very few people buy the one-person models.

Suppose a company that designs and makes clothes for kids brings out a whole line of sports clothes with extra-baggy shorts and extra-droopy tops. The officers of the company think "baggy"and "droopy" are what kids like most. But most kids are

WHAT'S THAT?
ELECTRONIC CERTIFICATES are commonly used to show proof of purchase for stocks, like sales receipts from a store. They stay in the computer file. To save money, some companies no longer provide paper confirmation for stock purchases.

WHAT'S THAT?
A VENTURE is an undertaking involving risk or uncertainty.

9

tired of baggy clothes and want to wear something different for a change, so no one buys the company's new shorts and tops.

The automobile and clothing manufacturing companies would both lose a great deal of money on their mistakes. Stockholders who owned a portion of the companies through their shares of stock would bear the risk. If management makes mistakes, its profits decrease, and investors lose money. Investors then sell their stocks, and the price of the stock goes down.

If the companies tried other ventures, and the next time designed products that became so popular that everyone would buy them, profits would go up. Shares of the stock would sell rapidly, and then the price of the stock would go up. In this case, the companies would make a great deal of money, and the stockholders, as partial owners of the companies, would make a nice profit. The price of stock changes from day to day, depending not only on how many shares of stock are bought and sold but also on how much money people are willing to pay for the stock.

## How many shares of its stock does a company sell?

**WHAT'S THAT?**
STOCK OPTIONS are plans that allow employees to purchase stock in the company for which they are working.

Company management decides how many shares are sold. Most managements decide how many shares of stock will be sold to the public, how many shares they will issue to their employees for **STOCK OPTIONS** and other sharing plans, and how many shares will be reserved for other purposes.

## How many shares in a company can one person buy?

All the shares offered in the marketplace can be bought. It depends on how much money a person wants to invest in the company.

Sometimes the board of directors of a company will decide to split stock. One reason is that the price of the stock may go too high. Splitting stock makes the stock more affordable and attracts more buyers. When a stock splits, buyers get an additional share for each share they own, like "Buy one slice of pizza, get one free." If you had 50 shares at $20 each, you now own 100 shares at $10 each.

## Is there more than one place to buy stocks?

Public companies must register their stocks with one exchange or marketplace. Many countries have their own market. The United States has the New York Stock Exchange (NYSE), the American Stock Exchange (AMEX), and the National Association of Securities Dealers Automated Quotation (NASDAQ). There are also nine smaller regional stock exchanges.

## Which exchange can I use?

In the U.S. stock market you can buy a specific company's stock only on the exchange with which that company is registered, but you can purchase on any exchange.

## What's my risk?

In investment terms, *risk* is how much you'd be willing to see the value of your security holdings move up or down. For example, suppose you were going to invest $1,000 in a company whose stock had the probability of suddenly rising in value because its product was in great demand. But you also stand a chance of its stock dropping, and of losing some of your investment because a better product just came on the market. This is the risk factor. The up-and-down movement of the price of a stock is called volatility. Risky or **VOLATILE STOCKS** offer the possibility of a greater return. This is the reward for taking a greater risk.

**WHAT'S THAT?** VOLATILE STOCKS often register sharp increases and decreases in their prices. A stock with volatility is one that is subject to frequent ups and downs.

# How can I find out if the value of my stock is going up or down?

**WHAT'S THAT?**
TRACKING a stock means checking its selling price and its price-earnings (P/E) ratio, which we'll tell you more about in Chapter Four.

You can track your stock through the newspaper listings each day. It is even easier to track performance through the Internet, since you can check it at any time of the day or night. **TRACKING** can be done as often as desired.

# What kind of information can people interested in stocks find on the Internet?

You can find companies' annual reports and earnings estimates as well as other information about their operations. A number of online brokers offer recommendations.

There are many Web sites for young people who are interested in stocks. For example, Salomon Smith Barney's Young Investors Network (http://www.salomonsmithbarney.com/yin) gives you information about kid-friendly companies, such as Tommy Hilfiger and McDonald's. They offer material to help you set your own goals for what you want out of life and to design a personalized plan to get there. They also hold contests for young people who want to compete in a portfolio game without investing real money.

ThinkQuest (www.thinkquest.org) also conducts a free stock-market game (http://library.think-quest.org/3096/), and gives advice on why and how to invest. It also lists kid-friendly companies.

Young Biz.com (www.youngbiz.com) offers daily performance updates on Nike, Disney, and McDonald's. It, too, offers a stock market game in which young people all over the world can compete for prizes.

*Kiplinger's Personal Finance* magazine teaches about the stock market through the Kids and Money section on their Web site (www.kiplinger.com/managing/kids/).

## Just for Fun

Pick one of these Web sites, or another you've heard about, and try it out. A stock rarely stays at the same selling price every day. Sometimes the changes are very small; the stock might be up or down just a few cents. Sometimes the changes are larger. Below is a chart of Disney stock for a four-year period.

You can chart, or track, a stock, too. Just for fun, write down the selling price of a stock every day for two weeks from a company whose products you like— Campbell's Soups, Wendy's, Nike, or maybe Hershey. Then, using graph paper, chart the activity of the stock.

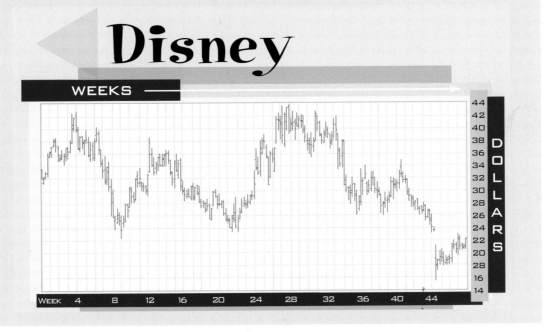

# 2

# Piggy Banks to Government Bonds

## There are a number of ways to invest your money.

In the Introduction we mentioned placing your money in piggy banks, savings accounts in banks, and the stock market. Piggy banks are fine for holding your pocket change in a safe place, but money in a piggy bank will earn zero **INTEREST**. Piggy banks are for saving, not investing. If you are really interested in making money, then you should let your money work for you.

When you deposit money in a savings account at a bank, you are allowing the bank to use your money to generate more money for itself. You can add money to this savings account, or you can take money out at any time. In exchange for the use of your funds, banks pay you interest. Interest on a savings account is usually low, because the bank does not know how long you will keep your money in the account. Therefore, they do not know how long they will be able to use your money. Banks lend money to individuals and businesses and charge borrowers interest on these loans. The bank's profit is the difference between what borrowers pay the bank in interest and the interest the bank pays to you for the use of your money.

## Let's talk about compound interest.

Compound interest is the sum paid on both the money you invested and the interest that has been added to it. Suppose you

**WHAT'S THAT?**
INTEREST is the money paid to people for the temporary use of their money.

put $1,000 into a savings account that pays you 4 percent interest, compounded yearly. At the end of the year your investment will be worth $1,040 ($1,000 x .04 = $40; $40 + $1,000 = $1,040). At the end of the second year, however, your investment will be worth $1,081.60. Where did the extra $1.60 come from? The 4 percent interest was paid on the entire amount, so the $1.60 is the interest paid on the extra $40. The third year's investment, which includes interest on the $1,000 and the $81.60, will amount to $1,124.86.

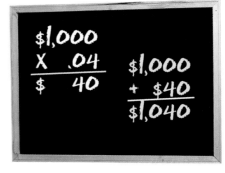

## Protected by the U.S. Government.

The U.S. government insures the money you have placed in a checking or savings account under the Federal Deposit Insurance Corporation (FDIC), so you are protected if the bank fails. There is little or no risk to your money in a bank account, but these accounts have a very low rate of growth.

## Are they playing your song?

Usually you can get a higher rate of interest from a bank if you put your money into a long-term CD. No, this CD does not contain the music you like. Same initials, but different tune. CD stands for certificate of deposit. When you invest your funds in a certificate of deposit, you agree to let the bank keep your money (a minimum of $1,000) for a certain amount of time, such as six months, a year, or several years at a specified rate of interest. You can't take your money out of the CD without paying a **PENALTY**. Because the bank can count on using your money for a specified time, it will pay you a slightly higher rate of interest than it would have paid for your money in a savings account.

**WHAT'S THAT?**
PENALTY is the interest you give up that would have been yours if you had left your money in the CD for the agreed-upon amount of time.

15

## What does the government offer investors?

Just like banks, the U.S. government also wants to use your money, so you can invest in Treasury notes, Treasury bonds, Treasury bills, and United States savings bonds, and earn interest.

Treasury notes and Treasury bonds are sold at $1,000 each. You pay $1,000 when you buy them, and they are worth exactly that when they reach **MATURITY**, but every six months you are paid interest on your investment. Treasury notes mature in one to ten years, depending on how long you agree to let the government use your money. Treasury bonds are sold for periods longer than ten years.

Treasury bills and U.S. savings bonds are sold at a discount, which means you pay less for them than their face value—what they are worth. Treasury bills at maturity are worth at least $10,000, and U.S. savings bonds at least $50. Interest on this type of loan to the government is included in the payment of the full amount of the bills or bonds at maturity. Treasury bills reach maturity in less than a year—many of them in just a few months. U.S. savings bonds usually reach their maturity date in ten years.

## How does the stock market compare with such investments?

The stock market offers opportunity to people who hope to get higher returns on their investments. But people who invest in stocks must be willing to take a few risks in order to make their money grow.

Are you one of these people?

Let's find out.

**WHAT'S THAT?**
MATURITY DATE is the agreed-upon time at which the money you paid for the bond must be returned to you. If you buy a T-note with a maturity date of one year, the last day of that period is the maturity date.

Yld   Sales
% P/E 100s High Low

52-Week
High Low Stock   Div

*[stock market listing graphic]*

# Just for Fun

Take a poll among your family and friends.
Ask them if they would be more likely to put
$100 into a risky investment if they thought
they could get a greater return, or if they
would rather protect their money
in an investment with a safer, lower return.
Which wins in popularity?
Risk or safety?

CHAPTER **3**

# What Type of Investment Is Best for You?

## Pete Pretend

Pete Pretend loves to go fishing with his grandfather, and his grandfather loves to talk to Pete about when he was a boy.

"My parents struggled through the Great Depression," Grandpa often says. "The stock market failed, people lost everything they owned, and the country was in really bad shape. I was just a boy, but I learned my lessons well. I've never trusted the stock market."

Grandpa knows that deposits in banks are insured, but he's even a little leery about trusting them with his money. "Sock your money away," he cautions Pete. "My mother—and a lot of people like her—used to tie their savings in an old sock and hide it. That's where the expression 'sock it away' came from."

Pete asks his dad, "Is Grandpa right? Should I just hide whatever money I save to keep it safe?"

Pete's father smiles. "Your grandpa's parents were afraid of losing what little money they had when he was young. That was before Congress established the Securities and Exchange Commission to regulate the stock market and protect investors. However, my advice to you is to invest with as little risk as possible. Put your money into savings accounts and government bonds. The interest they'll yield will be low, but it will be steady and protected."

At school Pete's teacher tells them they're going to join other schools throughout the country to play the national Stock Market Game, sponsored by local newspapers. They'll form teams, and each team will receive a make-believe $100,000 to invest in stocks. They'll learn to read the newspaper financial pages, study the growth rate of stocks, and make pretend investments. At the end of two months, they'll compare what they've earned and see how much their original investment has grown.

Pete learns with his teammates, and he's excited when a particular stock he has picked grows even more than he hoped. But the game makes Pete very uncomfortable. He doesn't like taking the risks some of his teammates are comfortable with. He'll be glad when the stock market game is over.

## Marcie Makebelieve

Marcie Makebelieve is always the first in her class to become involved in anything interesting that's going on. In one week she auditioned for a part in the school play, volunteered to work at the "Dunk the Principal" booth at the school carnival, and talked her best friend into signing up with her for a three-legged race.

Marcie likes to be the first in her class to see a new movie. She loves to read scary mystery stories, and whenever her family visits a restaurant, Marcie tries some new food she's never eaten before.

When Marcie's Aunt Alice asks her what she'd like to be when she grows up, Marcie answers, "I can't decide whether to be an astronaut or a movie star." Aunt Alice looks surprised. "Those are both very difficult jobs to get," she says. "Most people who try for them don't make it."

Marcie just smiles. "It doesn't hurt to try," she says.

When Marcie's teacher explains the Stock Market Game to her class, Marcie jumps up in excitement. Investing $100,000? Wow!

It doesn't matter that it's just play money. This is a great game. It's going to be fun. Marcie is sure her team is going to beat all the others. She can hardly wait to begin.

## Frankie Fictional

Frankie Fictional loves to play baseball. He'd rather play baseball than do anything else. But there is always homework to be done, and his parents have assigned certain household chores to Frankie and his brother and sister.

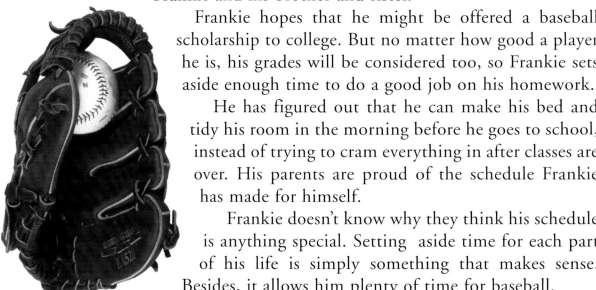

Frankie hopes that he might be offered a baseball scholarship to college. But no matter how good a player he is, his grades will be considered too, so Frankie sets aside enough time to do a good job on his homework.

He has figured out that he can make his bed and tidy his room in the morning before he goes to school, instead of trying to cram everything in after classes are over. His parents are proud of the schedule Frankie has made for himself.

Frankie doesn't know why they think his schedule is anything special. Setting aside time for each part of his life is simply something that makes sense. Besides, it allows him plenty of time for baseball.

Frankie is intrigued when his teacher tells the class about the Stock Market Game. His father invests in the stock market, so Frankie plans to ask him for advice. He's heard his dad talk to his mom about high-risk stocks, growth stocks, and blue chip stocks. Frankie would like a kind of balance in his team's investments. He doesn't care if his team "makes more money" than the others. He's more interested in investing in stocks that will bring in a nice, steady profit through growth and dividends. Frankie looks forward to beginning the game.

# How should we advise our fictional characters when it comes to stock market investments?

Pete is obviously going to be uncomfortable when it comes to taking risks. Pete will learn the benefits of investing in stocks, but he will want to encourage his team members to stick to conservative investments with long-range goals in mind.

Marcie is definitely a risk-taker. Her team may make quite a bit of money with investments if they take her advice. On the other hand, some of their investments may be so high risk that they "lose money." Overall, however, Marcie is going to enjoy the ups and accept the downs, because she feels the chance of becoming rich is worth the risk.

Frankie is a moderate investor. He doesn't mind taking a few risks, but on the whole he is going to convince his team to study the stocks they "buy" and have a pretty good idea of their potential.

## Just for Fun

How do you feel about investing? Answer the questions below and you may discover if you are a conservative investor, a risk taker, or a moderate investor.

1. Do you wait to go to a movie until you have read the reviews and at least two friends have already seen it and liked it?
2. Do you hate it when your mom has made something new for dinner and you don't know what's in it?
3. Do you insist on getting to school extra early on a day there's going to be a test because you want to make sure you're not late?
4. Do you still have money from previous birthdays stuffed in a piggy bank?
5. Do you go to the same camp every summer and pass up things that might be new and interesting because they make you feel uncomfortable?

**Then you are like Pete Pretend.**

1. Do you daydream about someday living in a beach house in the movie colony in Malibu, California?
2. Do you sometimes spend your entire allowance on a new item of clothing or a shoe fad because you're sure it's going to be popular and you want to be the first to be seen in it?
3. Do you fill out and mail in every sweepstakes contest entry blank you can find? You're not concerned with how much money you're spending for postage because you think that since someone has to win, it might as well be you.
4. Do you sometimes take dares, like who can eat a dish of ice cream the fastest, because you convince yourself that this time you won't get a headache?
5. Do you love to read mystery stories because they're the most exciting? And do you sometimes even write your own?

Then you are like Marcie Makebelieve.

1. Do you keep a calendar or notebook in which you keep track of tests or reports that are coming up, so you'll be sure to have plenty of time to prepare for them?
2. Do you like to try out different positions on a ball team because teamwork is more fun than trying to be a star?
3. Do you like to make your own plans, saving part of each allowance for a new bike, instead of hoping that eventually Grandma will start thinking about a bike as a birthday present?
4. Do you think ahead, already wondering what university you might want to attend? Or what profession you might want to enter?
5. Do you have as much fun with sandlot ball as with Little League? With a backyard picnic as with a downtown fireworks celebration? With reading a really good book as with going to a horror movie with friends?

Then you are like Frankie Fictional.

# How to Crack the Code

## 4

**Pete:** Crack a code? This sounds like a mystery.

**Marcie:** It's not a mystery if you know what it means. Come on.

**Frankie:** I love cracking codes.

Looking at the financial news in a newspaper, on television, or on a Web site can be overwhelming. Abbreviations and symbols seem to create a code that, at first glance, looks like a strange language. However, the stock market code is really much easier to understand than a different language.

Every stock has a *ticker symbol.* A ticker symbol is simply a short name, like a nickname. For example, just like Katie for Katherine or Nick for Nicholas, the stock market symbols on the Internet list KO or CCE for Coca-Cola and GM for General Motors. Shorter company names, such as Kmart (KM), Gap (GPS), and Disney (DIS) are abbreviated, too. The newspaper, however, uses different symbols: CocaCl for Coca-Cola, and GenMotr for General Motors. Kmart, Gap, and Disney are listed under their full names.

## The Code

Where is the stock traded? On the NASDAQ, AMEX, or the New York Stock Exchange? You can find listings online, in your newspaper, or in *The Wall Street Journal.* Stocks are listed in alphabetical order within the entries for each specific stock exchange.

Some listings may be less complete than others, but here are the headings naming the information in the listings:

# Today's Financial Times

| 52 Week | | | | Yld | | | | | | | |
| High | Low | Stock | Dividend | % | P/E | Sales | High | Low | Last | Change |

**52 WEEK HIGH/LOW:** These figures show the highest and the lowest prices for the stock in 52 weeks in dollars and cents.

**STOCK:** The abbreviated name of each company.

**DIVIDEND:** The amount of money the company has paid stockholders in the last year on each share of stock. If this area has three dots (. . .), the stock did not pay any dividends.

> Marcie: Shouldn't all the stocks I buy pay dividends?
>
> Frankie: No. Not all stocks pay dividends. My father told me that often new companies pay no or very low dividends while they're getting started.

**YLD%:** Yield percentage. This shows the dividends as a percentage of a stock's price. For example, if a stock costs $40 a share and pays a $4 dividend, the yield percentage is 10.

**P/E:** Price/Earnings ratio. This is one way to evaluate a stock. The P/E divides the price of the share by the company's earnings per share. For example, suppose a company earned a profit of $1 million, and the company and its shareholders together owned 200,000 shares of stock. The earnings are divided by the shares outstanding, at $5 a share. Next, the price paid for each share of stock—let's say $20—is divided by the $5, for a figure of 4. The price/earnings ratio is 4.

*Pete: Hey! That math is easy.*

A high P/E number means that investors are paying a high price for the stock relative to its earnings per share. The higher the ratio of the price to earnings, the greater the premium paid for the stock. Growth stocks have a high P/E because investors will pay more for a stock that is expected to rise quickly in value.

$1,000,000 PROFIT
÷ 200,000 SHARES
$5 PROFIT PER SHARE

$20 PRICE PER SHARE
÷ $5 PROFIT PER SHARE
4 P/E RATIO

**SALES (100/S) OR VOLUME:** This tells us how many shares of the stock were traded the day before. Add two zeros to the number to reach the actual figure. For example, 1=100.

**HIGH/LOW/LAST:** The highest, lowest, and last (closing) prices at which the stock traded the day before.

**CHANGE:** This number shows the difference between the price of the stock at closing the trading day before and the price at closing the day before that. A plus sign (+) means the price went up. A minus sign (-) means the price went down.

Here is an example in a shortened form giving information about Delta Air Lines (DAL):

| 52 Week High | Low | Stock | Sales | Last | Change |
|---|---|---|---|---|---|
| 58.31 | 43.56 | DAL | 4160 | 51.88 | +0.44 |

Now that you know the code, you can see the highest and lowest points at which Delta Air Line's stock was bought and sold during the previous 52 weeks. You know the volume of sales that took place the day before and what each share of stock sold for at the closing of the stock market. If you owned stock in Delta Air Lines, you would be very happy to see that the price rose nicely from the day before.

Pete: That's the kind of stock I want to buy— stock that makes a profit.

You can find ticker symbols and quotes on the Internet through many commercial Web sites. For example, PC Quote has a monthly or yearly charge for its services, but it also offers a few free services, which include showing the ticker symbols and current stock prices you ask for. The New York Stock Exchange (NYSE) site also offers symbol look-up, current price, and company information.

Your parents may already be using one of two software programs designed for their personal finances, including bank transactions. One is Microsoft Money. The other is Quicken Deluxe, which can be purchased through www.Quicken.com. These programs also offer Internet trading information and stock profiles from the past few years. Perhaps you can track the performance of a stock in which you're interested.

## What are the different types of stock?

*Common stock* is stock issued by corporations that give you a portion of ownership in the companies. If you own 100 shares of a company that has 100,000 shares outstanding, you own 1/1,000 of that company. Common stocks carry a risk. The profit for these stocks is influenced by the financial success or loss of the corporation. Shareholders have voting rights in proportion to the number of shares they own.

*Preferred stock* also gives investors ownership in a company, but not voting rights. While the **DIVIDENDS** paid on common stock

**WHAT'S THAT?**
A company shares profits with its stockholders through DIVIDENDS, or regular payments to stockholders. Each share earns the same dollar amount. For example, if the dividend is $1 a share and you own 100 shares, then your dividend is $100.

can fluctuate, the dividends paid on preferred stock are set at the time the stock is issued.

Marcie: I know there are two things I can do with dividends. I can take the money from the dividend in a cash payment to spend, or I can reinvest the dividends in the same company and receive more shares. Reinvesting my money makes sense to me. In that way my investment will grow faster.

*Income stock* is a name given to common stocks that pay high dividends on a regular or **QUARTERLY** basis, like an income from a steady job. A few examples of income-producing stock would be electric or telephone company stock. If you can't or don't want to take a big risk, stocks like these are a good choice for you. Sometimes value stocks are considered income stocks because they pay high dividends, but not all value stocks pay high dividends.

Pete: Those are my kind of stocks.

*Growth stocks* pay little or no dividends. The companies usually reinvest the surpluses in the company. Investors share in the company's growth through any increase in share prices. These stocks are more risky and should be held **LONG TERM**. Some companies have potential, and the stocks perform well, so the investor makes money. Other companies are not stable. The stocks may decrease in price, and the investor will lose money.

Frankie: People who like growth stocks should keep a close eye on their stocks. They can check

**WHAT'S THAT?**
QUARTERLY PAYMENTS from income stocks are issued every three months.

**WHAT'S THAT?**
Stocks held LONG TERM are those that are meant to be held by an investor for a number of years. The price of the stock may drop on occasion during this time, but quite often the stock will recover, rise, and provide a nice profit in the long run.

them at any time on the Internet.

*Blue-chip stocks* are stocks of large companies that have been in business for years and have demonstrated financial strength. Disney and McDonald's are examples of blue-chip stocks.

**Pete:** Just what I said. My kind of stock.

*Small-cap,* or small capitalization, *stocks* are stocks of companies with less than $5 billion in **MARKET CAPITALIZATION**. Small-cap companies can sometimes grow rapidly into large-cap companies. An example is Microsoft. When Bill Gates first began Microsoft, he had such a small company that he worked in his garage. Today, it is one of the world's largest companies.

**Marcie:** My aunt told me that the early Wal-Mart employees who right from the beginning kept buying stock in the company are now millionaires.

*Large-cap,* or large capitalization, *stocks* are stocks of companies with more than $5 billion in market capitalization. For example, General Electric and AT&T are large-cap companies.

## What is a mutual fund?

There are two kinds of mutual funds: open-end and closed-end. In open-end mutual funds, many investors buy shares in a fund, which is a collection of stocks and/or bonds, called a portfolio. A portfolio manager uses investors' money to buy stocks and bonds, and all the investors share in the portfolio. Instead of owning just a few stocks, each investor can share in

**WHAT'S THAT?**
MARKET CAPITALIZATION (MC) is the market value of all the company's outstanding shares. MC is equal to the price per share times the number of shares outstanding. For example, a $10 stock with 10,000 shares outstanding would have a market cap of $100,000. (MC = $10 x 10,000 = $100,000.)

$10 STOCK
X 10,000 SHARES
$100,000 MARKET CAP

many. This means that an investor's money is spread over stock in many companies.

Pete:  That sounds a lot safer.

Open-end mutual funds can be purchased from brokers or the mutual fund companies themselves. Many investors with a small amount of money choose to invest in mutual funds because they offer the chance to share in the risks and rewards of a large number of stocks.

Sometimes there are a great many investors in open-end mutual funds; sometimes there aren't very many. The portfolio manager must constantly try to balance the activity in the fund. Closed-end mutual funds, in order to avoid this problem, issue only a fixed number of shares, determined by the mutual fund's portfolio manager.

| | High | Low | Last | |
|---|---|---|---|---|
| | | | | Ch |
| 3 | 26 | 24¹³⁄₁₆ | 25¼ | |
| 0 | 25 | 23⅛ | 24⅜ | |
| 4 | 50¾ | 45¾ | 46⅜ | |
| 1 | 15¹¹⁄₁₆ | 14¾ | 15³⁄₁₆ | + |
| 1 | 139¾ | 127¹¹⁄₁₆ | 136⅛ | +4 |
| 6 | 21¾ | 21¹⁄₁₆ | 21¼ | + |
| 7 | 26⅛ | 23 | 23¹¹⁄₁₆ | -1 |
| 5 | 109 | 102¾ | 103³⁄₁₆ | -5 |
| 7 | 22⁷⁄₁₆ | 21⅜ | 21¹¹⁄₁₆ | + |
| 3 | 42 | 40⅜ | 40¾ | -1 |
| 2 | 92⁹⁄₁₆ | 89⅜ | 89¹³⁄₁₆ | -1 |
| 9 | 49¹⁄₁₆ | 46¾ | 48½ | |
| 4 | 50¾ | 48¹⁄₁₆ | 50⅜ | + |

In open-end and closed-end mutual funds, investors rely on professional portfolio managers to choose their stocks. Millions of investors pool their money, but they have no say in the stocks or bonds the portfolio manager picks.

Marcie:  I'd rather study the stocks and pick them myself.

Pete:  I wouldn't. I'd like an expert to do it for me.

Frankie:  On TV news we keep hearing about bull markets, bear markets, and the Dow Jones Industrial Average. What are they talking about?

## A Bull Market

This term describes a market with an upward trend. Horns point up on a bull, so the market is going up. Investments go from low to high and look as if they will continue to rise. The bull lifts up his horns and takes the stock market with him.

## A Bear Market

This term describes a market with a downward trend. The bear's paws point down, so the market is headed down. When prices are falling, it is sometimes seen as a good time to buy stock. When stocks are bought at their lowest prices, any rise in their price means a profit for investors.

> **Frankie:** I've heard the old saying, "Buy low, sell high."
>
> **Pete:** That's what everybody wants to do. It doesn't mean it's going to happen.

## The Dow Jones Industrial Average

The Dow Jones Industrial Average is an indicator of how the entire stock market is performing, based on the price of a certain

thirty blue-chip stocks. This system was developed in 1896 by journalist Charles H. Dow, who chose thirty high-quality stocks that had strong histories and paid dividends consistently. Their activity represents how well or how poorly the market does each day. To reflect current conditions, the Index sometimes replaces a stock with another, more representative one. Online brokers may list them, or go directly to the Dow Jones Web site (www.dowjones.com).

There are other stock-market indicators, such as the Standard & Poor's 500 Index, which tracks 500 common stocks to indicate what the broader stock market is doing. Still other indicators, such as the Dow Jones Utility Average, measure certain sectors or industries.

## What are capital gains?

Capital gains are profits from the sale of an investment, such as stock shares. The U.S. government collects taxes on capital gains. The amount you are taxed depends on your parents' **TAX BRACKET** until you reach the age of fourteen. Keep all your records in one safe place to use when preparing your income-tax return. Like dividends, you can use capital gains to spend at the moment, or you can reinvest these profits in the stock market.

**WHAT'S THAT?**
TAX BRACKETS are ranges on the scale of income, according to how much money you earned. The higher your total income for the year, the higher your tax bracket, and the more of your income will go to the U.S. Treasury to pay income taxes.

# Just for Fun

Compare the stock listings in a newspaper, on TV (try CNN), and on a Web site.
Which are the most complete?
Which are easiest to follow?
Which gives you the information you need?

# NASDAQ NATIONAL MARKET

| 52-Week High | Low | Stock | Div | Yld % | P/E | Sales 100s | High | Low | Last | Chg |
|---|---|---|---|---|---|---|---|---|---|---|
| | | **A** | | | | | | | | |
| 2.25 | 0.22 | A Consul | ... | ... | dd | 1 | 0.30 | 0.30 | 0.30 | ... |
| 20.35 | 11.17 | AAON s | ... | ... | 13 | 18 | 20.50 | 20.00 | 20.00 | −0.80 |
| 14.90 | 1.86 | AB Watl | ... | ... | dd | 237 | 2.06 | 1.95 | 1.98 | −0.04 |
| 14.00 | 9.13 | ABC Bcp | .48 | 3.5 | 13 | 89 | 13.70 | 13.65 | 13.65 | −0.15 |
| 34.00 | 7.94 | AC Moore | ... | ... | 35 | 382 | 31.75 | 29.60 | 29.88 | −0.07 |

| 52-Week High | Low | Stock | Div | Yld % | P/E | Sales 100s | High | Low |
|---|---|---|---|---|---|---|---|---|
| 24.50 | 17.50 | AllncFnc | .76 f | 3.2 | 14 | 1 | 23.95 | 23.95 |
| 33.60 | 4.38 | AlliGam s | ... | ... | 28 | 5572 | 32.48 | 31.19 |
| 40.63 | 2.66 | AlianPh rs | ... | ... | ... | 398 | 3.02 | 2.91 |
| 29.99 | 17.19 | AllnceRs n | 2.00 | 7.4 | 22 | 199 | 27.53 | 26.90 |
| 16.50 | 6.24 | AllianSemi | ... | ... | dd | 5788 | 11.80 | 11.39 |
| 3.95 | 2.97 | AldHlPd | ... | ... | cc | 5 | 3.60 | 3.60 |
| 4.50 | 0.06 | AllRiser n | ... | ... | dd | 4466 | 0.20 | 0.17 |
| 8.69 | 4.25 | AllosThera | ... | ... | dd | 123 | 6.12 | 6.05 |

31

CHAPTER **5**

# Setting Up a Portfolio

## What's a portfolio?

When you invest in the stock market your parents and your financial adviser will create a portfolio with you. A portfolio is the collection of all your financial assets. It might include money you keep in a savings account, a U.S. savings bond you received for a

birthday present from your aunt and uncle, and investments in stocks and/or mutual funds. These are listed by dates, so you and your parents know your investments' total value at specific times. You can check your portfolio and record the amounts for each item weekly, monthly, or even annually.

A *balanced portfolio* means that your investments are not all of one kind. You might have a few small-cap, volatile stocks. To balance them, you'd want some steady blue-chip stocks and a few government bonds. Low-risk investments balance high-risk ones. Keep in mind your goals and the time in which you hope to reach them. These factors will also help you decide which stocks to include in your portfolio.

## What should you do before creating your portfolio?

Like Pete, Marcie, and Frankie, you have learned what your investment style is. Now you must learn what kinds of stocks and bonds you want in your portfolio. You must also decide how much money you want to invest. How much can you afford to lose? Should you try **HIGH RISK/HIGH RETURN** stocks or more secure stocks?

Marcie: High risk/high return for me!

Pete: Not for me. I want stock that's more secure.

Frankie: I might like a portfolio with a little of both types of stock in it. I'll have to give it some thought.

Make a list of ten stocks in which you're interested. Consider some of these questions. Do you like computers, cars, or movies? Did your school buy new computers? What kind were they? What brands of clothes are you and your friends wearing? What are the most popular items right now?

Then take the next step—research. Take a look at the companies that make these products. Narrow your choice to specific stocks. Read the financial section of the newspaper, watch television newscasts, and check financial Web sites. How much profit did a particular company make last year? If it shows gains, chances are it is a good investment. Are the companies in which you are interested financially stable? Do the companies you like provide products or services that will be used and needed in the future? These are good signs that can encourage you to buy their stock. Are you reading news reports that a company is involved in a lawsuit or might be sold? These are signs that warn you not to buy.

Also check on the company's competition. Who are the company's major competitors? How strong are they? Is there room for many competitors in its field? The Gap, Levi's, and Tommy

Hilfiger are all successful with their clothing—and stock.

Some companies produce a variety of products. Do you know all the products? Are there any to which you might object? Do these products sell well? Do they have active competition from other companies making similar products? Are the products priced right? Research the companies in which you're interested through their published reports or through the Internet.

Many brokerage firms also offer online research on their Web sites without requiring users to open trading accounts. You can get the names of these firms by going into Web sites whose purpose is to guide you to online brokerage sites. Check out Wall Street Directory (www.wsdinc.com), Investorguide (www.investorguide.com), or Invest-O-Rama (www.investo-rama.com), in addition to Quicken (www.quicken.com) and MoneyCentral Investor (moneycentral.msn.com/investor/).

## Read each company's annual report.

Check out companies' annual reports about their production and earnings. You might be able to get a copy of their reports at your public library, or you can read them on the Internet. The reports will show the company's financial history for the past five years. If you see a steady increase in a company's profit, it shows that it's strong, and that strength is likely to continue.

However, you may see that profit has been low because the company has spent a great deal of money in research, in redesigning its products, or in expanding its number of stores, working to achieve more growth and profit in the future. If it looks as if the company's expenditures, or expenses, will result in greater profits, then the stock may be a very good buy.

A company's annual report will probably also contain a forecast for its growth during the next five years. Does it look promising? If everything about that company's stock looks good, then take the next step.

## Track each of your stock picks for two months.

Make a chart of each day's stock price over a period of time. This can give you a good picture of how the stock is performing. If the selling price fluctuates a great deal, and you are not interested in volatile stocks, you can drop a stock of this type from your list. If your list of stocks seems too conservative, or low risk, then you might think of adding a more volatile stock. Keep your goals in mind as you try to construct a balanced portfolio.

## Just for Fun

Create four portfolios of real stocks listed
in the financial pages or on the Internet.
One portfolio of five stocks should be chosen for
Pete Pretend, who is more conservative about investing.
One should be for Marcie Makebelieve,
who has let us know she's a real risk-taker
and wants high-return stocks.
One should be for Frankie Fictional,
who likes a portfolio of a variety of stocks.
And the fourth is for you,
with your own choice of five stocks.
Track these portfolios each day for two weeks. Which
was the best choice? Which is earning the most money?

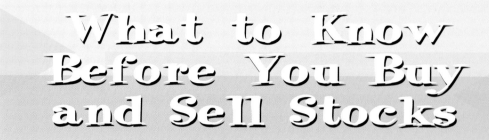

CHAPTER

# 6 What to Know Before You Buy and Sell Stocks

## What about stockbrokers?

Stockbrokers are people who take many tests and earn a license so that they can sell and buy stocks for investors who hire them to do so. Most stockbrokers work for full-service broker/dealer firms. These are financial-services companies that answer all your investing questions and then buy or sell stock for you. You can also find such firms on the Internet. Full-service broker/dealer firms and full-service brokers charge commissions for trading and give clients all the information they need to make intelligent choices when they are ready to invest.

Stockbrokers research the companies that issue stock. They keep informed about trends in the market, new and established companies, and the foreign market. With this knowledge they help you and your parents set your individual goals.

## How do you choose a stockbroker?

The easiest way to choose a stockbroker is to ask your family or friends who they would recommend.

Marcie: My father has a stockbroker. She was recommended by one of his friends. But before my father chose her to invest his money, he asked her a lot of questions.

Since it is your money, when you and your parents interview the stockbroker, don't be shy about asking questions, such as:

- What is your education?
- How much experience have you had?
- What is your performance track record?
- What type of stocks do you usually recommend? Large cap, small cap, growth, or value?

Make sure he or she takes part in the profession's continuing education, keeps up with the market and the particular stocks she is recommending, and gives you references. You want to build a long-term investment portfolio and not a trading account, so it's important that she listen to you. Talk to her about your goals. You want to work with someone who understands them and will recommend the kind of stock that you feel comfortable with. The stockbroker should have your best interests in mind. Your goals, money, and investments should be as important to your stockbroker as they are to you.

If you don't have a referral from someone, call a brokerage firm and ask the manager of the branch office to recommend someone. Become acquainted, then interview him with these same, important questions.

Marcie: My father's saving for his retirement, but my goal is to earn lots of money to help pay my college tuition in a few years.

## What does a stockbroker do?

Stockbrokers plan and offer guidance on stock and bond portfolios. With the authorization of their clients, stockbrokers buy and sell stocks to improve returns and make more money for them.

WHAT'S THAT?
COMMISSION
is the percent-
age of the buy-
ing or selling
price of stock
paid to the
broker.

Stockbrokers are paid a **COMMISSION** or fee for making trades (buying and selling).

Until 1975 brokers were regulated and had to charge the same commissions and fees. But firms wanted to be able to compete with each other in terms of what services they offered and what they charged. So the regulation was changed. Some companies began calling themselves discount brokers.

Pete: Discount? I'm always interested in a discount.

## What is a discount broker?

Have you ever been to a gas station where the customers pump the gas and check the air in the tires themselves? No frills. The discount broker operates on this principle. You do all the research on the stocks, and you receive no advice about when to buy or sell. Basically, all the responsibility is yours. You tell the broker what stocks to buy or sell for you.

However, with discount brokers the commission is lower than with full-service brokers. Discount brokers are available twenty-four hours a day, so, when you telephone, you may speak or input to a machine, not a person. If you have plenty of time to track stocks and you enjoy doing so, this may be a good option for you.

There are many reputable discount brokers on the Internet, such as Charles Schwab & Company, Inc. (www.schwab.com), Waterhouse Securities (www.webbroker.com), and Empire Financial Group (www.empirenow.com). They charge low fees, and some require low minimum deposits.

Deep-discount brokers are the least expensive of all. They do not offer advice or recommendations, and your dealings are only with a computer, not a person who might answer questions or provide explanations. Some deep-discount online brokers are

Ameritrade (www.ameritrade.com), E*Trade (www.etrade.com), and InvestExpress (www.investexpress.com)

## What is a financial planner?

Financial planners deal with all aspects of personal finance. They work with clients on budgeting, investments, taxes, insurance, credit, real estate, estate planning, retirement, and college financing. The majority of financial planners work at an hourly rate, but some work on fees based on the amount of the assets that are involved. They are happy to work with you if you have $50 or if you have millions. They work one-on-one with their clients to formulate the client's goals.

**Pete:** Can you find a financial planner on the Internet?

**Frankie:** My uncle uses Quicken Financial Planner. That software teaches financial planning and has programs for setting your savings goals.

**Pete:** You mean it's a do-it-yourself?

**Frankie:** Not all by yourself. Their advisers give you a guide to follow.

## What is a portfolio manager of a mutual fund?

A mutual fund portfolio manager works for the mutual fund company. He is paid a salary plus a bonus that is dependent on the performance returns of the fund each year. He and the fund's chief investment strategist choose stocks and bonds to buy and sell within the mutual fund. The portfolio manager has his own research staff and receives the fastest, up-to-the-minute reports about the market. Each mutual fund is known for its specialized portfolio of stocks. Some include only the most dependable blue-chip stocks. Others try for faster growth stocks.

## Do you need a broker to buy mutual funds online?

Through your parents you can buy mutual funds directly from the fund company or from a broker. If you want to invest in mutual funds online, you can go to an online broker's Web site. If you are under eighteen years old, you are a minor and cannot sign legal documents. But your parents can register and open a custodial account for you. That means they can handle your investing for you. After your account is open, you can go into your broker's Web site at any time to check your investments.

## How can you avoid being scammed?

As in any business, there are a few people who are not honest. They offer investments that benefit only themselves, not their investors. They might try to assure you, through their telephone

calls, e-mail, or letters, that what they offer carries no risk and pays very high returns. They might insist that the return of your money is guaranteed, or that you have to act right away in order to get in on an investment, or that their offer is for only a few select people. If they do, you can be sure they are not reliable brokers.

You can investigate any brokerage firm by telephoning the Better Business Bureau in your area, or going into the BBB Web site (www.bbb.org). You can learn if there have been any complaints against the firm, how long it has been in business, and if any government agency has taken any action against it during the past three years.

If you receive offers that sound too good to be true, you can discover if they are fraudulent by contacting the Federal Trade Commission, the National Association of Securities Dealers, or the Securities and Exchange Commission. To find your local Securities Regulator, go to the North American Securities Administrators Association (NASAA) Web site (www.nasaa.org) and click on *FindRegulator*. Don't hesitate to ask about any firm if you have doubts. These organizations want to help you.

## Just for Fun

Our government does a good job of protecting investors from fraud. Discover what the United States Securities and Exchange Commission offers by going to their Web site (www.sec.gov). On the main page, under "Investor Information," you can click on *Check Out Brokers and Advisers* and *Complaint Center*.

The exchanges themselves also do their best to protect investors. As self-regulatory organizations, they work with the SEC to monitor each and every trade. And they ensure a fair and orderly marketplace for all investors. Visit www.nyse.com to learn more about how the New York Stock Exchange regulates its market.

CHAPTER 7

# Buying and Selling Stocks

## How do you place an order to buy or sell stocks?

After you've established a custodial account or engaged a broker, ordering a stock is as easy as ordering a pizza. It begins with a phone call.

**Pete:** Pizza? Is anybody else hungry?

**Marcie:** Why don't you save your money and buy stock in a pizza company?

Through your parents, you may ask your stockbroker to buy a certain stock at the best price set by the market-maker. This is called a *market order*. You can never be sure of the exact price you will pay because that price may change by the time your order is carried out. Market order is the most common method used by investors. It is simply buying or selling a specific number of stocks immediately at the best available price.

You may place a *limit order* for a certain stock at a price below the current asking price, then wait until the price of the stock drops to the price you specified. You may place it for one day, called a *day order*, or until you cancel it. This is called *GTC*, or good till canceled.

When you place an order for a stock, you ask your broker the current *bid price* for the stock. The bid price is the amount the buyer wants to pay for the stock. The *ask price* is the price set by the seller. The bid/ask prices are set by the market-makers based on the range of orders they receive. If you want to buy a stock, look at what other investors have bid (the lowest price). Then look at what sellers of stock are asking (the highest price). You can expect to pay something in between the two prices.

The difference between a stock's bid price and ask price is called a spread. The spread gives room to negotiate the price. Spreads are used as payments to market-makers and brokers when stock is traded. Stock prices are quoted in decimals, and a spread can be as little as one cent.

> **Pete:** If I bought stock in a pizza company, and my friends and I ate a lot of their pizza, it would help make the company more successful. And if it's more successful, the value of the stock will go up. Right?
>
> **Frankie:** Right.
>
> **Pete:** Who wants pepperoni?

## How do you buy stocks through the stock exchange in foreign countries?

Foreign companies, like U.S. companies, issue stock in order to raise capital. There are stock exchanges in London, Paris, Tokyo, and many other foreign financial centers. Many stockbrokers in the United States can trade on foreign stock exchanges, but many foreign stocks are registered with the Securities and Exchange Commission and are listed on the New York and American Stock Exchanges and NASDAQ, so their stock is easy to buy.

The shares of non-U.S. stocks take the form of an American depositary receipt, or ADR. ADRs are securities issued by a U.S.

bank to represent the foreign shares held in trust by that bank. This process allows investors to buy and sell foreign shares. Some foreign stocks are considered to be high risk/high return. The most closely watched index tracking foreign stocks is the Morgan Stanley Capital International Europe, Australasia, Far East (EAFE) Index.

## Selling Stocks

The goal of investing in stock is to make a profit. Determining when the time is right to sell a stock is a tough decision. However, when you sell, there must be a buyer—someone who thinks it would be profitable to buy the stock. How do you know what to do? There are a few guidelines to help you decide.

Imagine that the stock you bought a year ago in the Zipper Tennis Shoe Company increased in value for seven months. After that, the stock has been slowly decreasing in value, and you notice that no one is wearing Zipper tennis shoes anymore. Now, before the value of the stock drops lower than your purchase price, might be a good time to sell.

Lately, though, you have read that a famous sports figure has just signed a contract to endorse a newly designed Zipper tennis shoe on television. There's a good chance that sales will increase greatly and the price of Zipper stock will rise. Now, while stock prices are low, may be a good time to buy more Zipper stock. You see that within one year Delta Air Lines stock went from a low of $37.51 to a high of $58.31. You also notice that in one day it had gone up from $43.56 to $51.88 ($8.32 a share). If you had bought the stock at $37.51, you would have seen a profitable rise, even if its value dipped now and then. But what if you had bought it at $50 and it had dropped? Here is where patience is helpful. Many successful stock investors believe in holding stock for long periods of time. If they have enough faith in a company to invest in its stock, they expect to see the stock become more valuable over time.

Most of the questions you asked when you were thinking of buying stock apply to selling stock, too.

**Frankie:** If I read a negative report about the company, I'd find out as much as I could about what the company was doing.

**Pete:** If the drop in the stock was temporary, okay. But I'd sell it if there had been a steady drop.

**Marcie:** There are lots of details to pay attention to. What if I heard that a stockholder with many shares suddenly sold her stock? I'd probably sell, too.

No matter what your reason for wanting to sell your stock, don't panic. Talk to your stockbroker. Many advisers recommend holding a stock for many years. A stock may temporarily drop, but in the long run, it may be more likely to make a profit for investors. Sometimes investors become frightened by a piece of news, such as the failure of a large company or a rise in interest rates. There is a time in investing when it is wise to **CUT YOUR LOSSES AND SELL** and invest in other stocks.

When the Federal Reserve raises interest rates, they charge the banks. The banks then pass this expense on to their customers by charging them more to borrow money. This means that a company's expenses are rising and its profits will be lower. This may

**WHAT'S THAT?** CUT YOUR LOSSES AND SELL. This is a phrase used by brokers that means: If your stocks continue to trade below the cost at which they were bought, it's a good idea to sell them and lose some money before they drop further.

lower the value of its stock. Also, if interest rates are high, some people tend to take their money from the stock market and invest in savings accounts, Treasury bonds, or other investments that pay interest. As a result, the stock market drops. Then the frightened investors rush to sell their stocks. In the long run, people who give in to panic decisions earn much less money in the stock market than those investors who hold their stock and wait for the stock market to settle down. You should always make an informed decision before you sell.

## Selling Mutual Funds

You can sell your mutual funds as easily as you can sell your stock in individual companies. If the fund in which you have invested is no longer growing and performing well, you might consider selling it and investing in a different mutual fund.

Pete: If the portfolio manager of the mutual fund adds too many volatile stocks, that will make me nervous. I'd want to sell that fund and invest in a more conservative fund.

Marcie: I'm just the opposite. I like volatile stocks. I'd be unhappy in a highly conservative, slow growing fund. I'd sell it and look for a mutual fund that suited me.

# Just for Fun

Take a poll among adults you know who own stock.
Ask what reasons they had for purchasing stock.
Was a particular stock recommended?
Was it stock in a company that
produced a favorite product?

Ask what reasons they had for selling stock.
Was there concern over
stock market changes?
Our country's economic situation?
A lack of interest in the
company's product?
Were these informed,
well-thought-out reasons?

## WHY THEY BOUGHT STOCKS

RECOMMENDED BY A FRIEND: ||||| ||||| ||||
MAKES A COOL PRODUCT: |
RESULT OF RESEARCH: ||||
HAD A CUTE NAME: |||
RELATIVES OWNED STOCK: ||||| ||
SAW IT DISCUSSED ON TV: ||
WAS IN THE NEWS RECENTLY: ||
THREW A DART: |
OTHER:

# 8

# Stocks and Your Long-Term Goals

## How can you make your money work for you?

Many young people hope to be able to go to college, so earning and saving money to help with paying college expenses is their primary goal. If you have your heart set on a college education, you should begin planning now. How many years will it be before you register at a college or university? Only six? Seven? Or eight?

Then let's think about how your money will work for you to help you reach this goal. Let's imagine that the income you want to put aside for your goal each year is $1,000—a combination of earnings received from babysitting, walking neighbors' dogs, feeding their fish, and watering their plants while they're on vacation, added to your allowance and birthday and holiday checks from your grandparents and favorite great aunt.

You could stuff a metal lockbox with this money and hide it under your bed. At the end of seven years you will have exactly $7,000. Lockboxes don't pay interest, so your money hasn't grown by a single penny.

You can also put your money into a savings account. Even though the interest is usually no higher than 3 percent, your savings will be compounded annually. After seven years your total interest will be approximately $892.05 if compounded annually. Add it to the $7,000 you deposited and it comes to $7,892.05. That's a nice step up from $7,000, but since **INFLATION** has been growing at about 3 to 3.5 percent each year, you will actually have lost money by accepting an interest rate lower than the inflation rate.

**WHAT'S THAT?**
INFLATION means that the cost of living rises over time. Each year everything from loaves of bread to new cars becomes more expensive.

Suppose you decide to put all your money into certificates of deposit, or CDs. The interest rate varies, but for the past few years has been staying close to 5 percent. In seven years you will have earned $1,549.12 in interest for a total of $8,549.12.

If you invest your money regularly in mutual funds or stocks, there is a good chance, based on past performance of the stock market, that your investments will earn a return of at least 10 percent. This would give you a total of approximately $10,435.89 at the end of seven years.

Frankie: Is that guaranteed? Or is there a risk?

Marcie: There's always a risk, but there's also a chance to get an even bigger return on your investment.

## What about the risk?

There is a certain amount of risk in almost any undertaking. However, some stocks are considered to be high risk, and some have a low risk factor. Blue-chip stocks have a steady, stable, long-term performance record, so the stock price is not volatile. That means blue-chip stocks are considered low risk. They also have a lower return than high-risk stocks.

Pete: I told you those were my kinds of stocks.

On the other hand, during the past few years some investors saw some Internet stocks soar to very high valuations, then suddenly plunge. If they sold their stocks when they were at their peak, the investors made a great deal of money. If they held their stocks through their drop in value, investors lost the money they had invested in them.

## Mutual Funds, T-Notes, IRAs, and More

Investing in mutual funds offers more diversification of a portfolio, which gives it a certain amount of safety. Therefore, many financial advisers recommend to young investors who are college bound that they invest in stocks through mutual-fund holdings. Then, two years before college, the principal, plus dividends, can be sold and put into Treasury notes.

T-notes set an interest rate on the value of the security and pay interest every six months. When the T-note reaches its maturity date, you receive the face value of the security. T-notes are backed by the U.S. government and are considered a completely safe investment. Depending on your tax bracket, you may not have to pay federal income taxes on the interest you earn from a T-note. The interest is exempt from state and local income taxes.

## What are other ways to pay for college?

Your parents can invest in an education IRA for you, which must be used for education only. This investment can be in stocks or mutual funds. As long as the money is used for qualified education expenses, such as tuition, books, fees, supplies, and room and board at an educational institution, it is free from federal income tax. Any funds from an education IRA account that are unused can be transferred to the educational account of another child within the family.

Frankie:  My grandfather gave me some money through the Uniform Gifts to Minors Act. Can I invest this in the stock market?

Yes. This money can be invested in the stock market. Its earnings will be taxed at your parents' rate until you are fourteen years old. Then it will be taxed at your own rate, usually 15 percent. Starting in 2001, the first $750 earned each year is tax-exempt. This figure continues to rise.

## What about Individual Retirement Accounts (IRAs)?

Your parents can invest in one for you if you earn less than $2,000 a year. However, you will have to keep your investment in the IRA until you are 59 years old—with only a few exceptions allowed, such as higher-education expenses—or pay a penalty.

## Just for Fun

Imagine that you have a part-time job in a fast-food restaurant. Your monthly earnings are $200. Figure out how much of this money you will use for clothing, entertainment, school, and living expenses. Then decide how much you can put aside each month to invest in the stock market.

STUFF **I REALLY** WANT

NEW CLOTHES FOR THE DANCE: $60
SHOES TO MATCH: $20
MOVIES WITH MY FRIENDS: $15
NEW MUSIC CD: $15
LOCKER MIRRORS: $12
TOTAL: $122
WHAT I EARN: $200
WHAT'S LEFT TO INVEST: $78

# Let's Talk About Balanced Portfolios

As they save, all investors should aim at eventually holding at least twelve to twenty stocks in their portfolios. By owning a number of stocks investors can diversify, taking less risk. Remember the old saying, "Don't put all your eggs in one basket." This caution also applies to the stock market, where diversification is very important. A practical way to diversify is to begin investing your money in mutual funds.

## What exactly does diversification mean?

Diversifying means putting your money into different types of stock. Invest in a number of companies that interest you. If one investment loses money, you still have others that might be profitable. You should feel comfortable with your portfolio, and your financial adviser or stockbroker will take your preferences into consideration when suggesting stocks for it.

Pete Pretend, who is super-cautious about investing in stocks, would be happiest buying stock in older, well-established companies that pay a dividend to shareholders. They'd suggest a stock like the fictional Light 'n Shine Electric Utility Company, which pays at least $2.50 in dividends annually for each share of stock. Pete knows that no matter how much the stock price goes up or down, he will get $2.50 per share paid to him each year—$0.63 each quarter.

Pete's portfolio would also include stock in the imaginary Great Blue Steel, Inc. He knows this is the largest producer of steel for autos, ships, buses, trains, and building supplies. They manufacture materials for which there is a constant need. The price of their stock will vary, depending on amount of production and amount of dividends paid, but overall should show a steady profit.

Pete can't wait until he's old enough to drive, and he has his eye on a special pickup truck manufactured by the imaginary Flintstone Motors. He's watched Flintstone stock, and seen the company continue to profit from their well-built cars, so he's happy that his portfolio will contain Flintstone Motors stock.

Marcie Makebelieve is a risk-taker, and she likes "hot stocks" of fictional companies such as NewThing.com, GamesForU.com, and Super Techno, Inc. Today it's the technology industry, but tomorrow Marcie will switch to whatever is temporarily leading the market. She'll do a lot of trading in her account and, as a result, her trading costs will increase, which will cut her profits.

Marcie's stockbroker advises her to balance her portfolio with some corporate bonds and blue-chip stocks. Marcie reluctantly takes her advice, but even with these stocks she's aggressive. She instructs her stockbroker to reinvest all earnings from these stocks back into the companies to increase her position. (This move increases her risk because she is putting all her profit back into the same companies.) She is, however, keeping her money working for her, instead of spending it.

Frankie Fictional takes a middle road and looks for a variety of stocks that will bring in a steady profit. At his stockbroker's recommendation, he invests in a basket of stocks spread over several different unrelated industries. They are moderately volatile but stable large-cap companies such as the imaginary Friendly Faces Bank, Jumping Jeans, Inc., and Phancy Pills and Potions. Frankie has invested in financial, retailing, and pharmaceutical stocks, covering a number of bases.

## How do the investment programs compare?

You created and tracked portfolios of real stock for Pete Pretend, Marcie Makebelieve, and Frankie Fictional. How do the portfolios compare with regard to earnings? Which person made the most profit from his or her investment? Which portfolio is close to what you might choose for yourself?

## Just for Fun

Set up a portfolio containing
stock in only one company.
Track it for two weeks.
Then compare it with the diversified
portfolios you created for Pete, Marcie,
Frankie, and yourself. What was the
result of not diversifying?

| Portfolio | Diversified | Start | 2 Weeks | Change |
|-----------|-------------|-------|---------|--------|
| Mine | No | 42.60 | 47.80 | 5.20 |
| Pete's | Yes | 67.90 | 80.90 | 13.00 |
| Marcie's | Yes | 50.60 | 80.20 | 29.60 |
| Frankie's | Yes | 77.70 | 77.50 | 0.20 |

Remember that Pete, Marcie, Frankie, and you are minors. You can't buy stocks yourself until you reach the age of eighteen, so your parents, grandparents, or guardians must do it for you through custodial accounts. Your stock investments will be based on teamwork. Together you can study the markets, read companies' annual reports, and ask for advice from your stockbroker or financial planner. Whether you invest with a stockbroker or on the Internet, you're going to do your best to make wise, well-thought-out decisions to make your money grow. You'll soon become an investor who is Stock Market Smart.

# For More Information

## Books

Bamford, Janet. *Street Wise: A Guide for Teen Investors.* Princeton, NJ: Bloomberg Press, 2000.

Brown, David, and Kassandra Bentley. *Getting Started in Online Investing.* New York: John Wiley and Sons, 1999.

Caes, Charles J. *The Young Zillionaire's Guide to the Stock Market.* New York: Rosen, 2000.

Heady, Christy. *The Complete Idiot's Guide to Making Money on Wall Street,* 2nd ed. New York: Alpha Books, 1998.

Karlitz, Gail, and Debbie Honig. *Growing Money: A Complete Investing Guide for Kids.* New York: Price Stern Sloan, 2001.

Liebowitz, Jay. *The Wall Street Wizard: Advice from a Savvy Teen Investor.* New York: Simon & Schuster, 2000.

Sindell, Kathleen. *Investing Online for Dummies,* 2nd ed. Foster City, CA: IDG Books Worldwide, 1999.

Walker, Emmanuel and Andrea. *Teenvestor.com: The Practical Investment Guide to Teens and Their Parents.* Nevada City, CA: Gateway, 2000.

# Games

**THE STOCK MARKET GAME** is a ten-week investment game for students in grades four through twelve and adults. Throughout the country newspapers sponsor students who work in teams to invest an imaginary $100,000 in companies whose stocks are traded on the New York Stock Exchange. In each locality the teams that make the most profit on their investments, along with their teachers, are honored at receptions and win cash awards and prizes.

# In Print

**TIME TO SAVE**, Merrill Lynch's educational packet for young people, includes **BRAIN QUEST**, a palm-sized set of cards with questions and answers on everything about money.

# Magazines

*Fortune, Business Week, Barron's, Money Magazine,* and *Forbes* are just a few of the many business and investment magazines that publish news and feature articles about the stock market.

# Newspapers

*The Wall Street Journal, USA Today*'s Money Section, *The New York Times* Business Section, and the business sections of many local newspapers provide stock quotes and charts, finance news, and the latest information about stocks. They may also have their own Web sites.

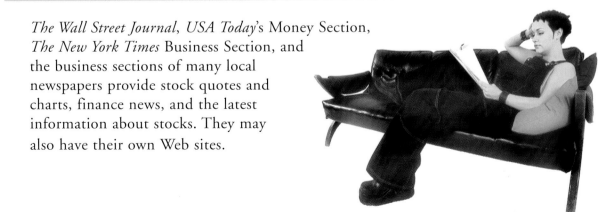

# Online

### INVEST WISELY
http://www.sec.gov/consumer/inws.htm
This Web site is designed by the Securities and
Exchange Commission (SEC) to inform beginning
investors and protect them from fraud.

### KIPLINGER'S PERSONAL FINANCE MAGAZINE
http://www.kiplinger.com/magazine/kids
This Web site has a "Kids and Money" section that teaches
the ways of the stock market.

### QUICKEN.COM
http://www.quicken.com
This Web site contains information on portfolio
management, along with the latest news on stocks and investing.

### SALOMON SMITH BARNEY'S YOUNG INVESTORS NETWORK
http://www.salomonsmithbarney.com/yin
This Web site includes information about youth-friendly
companies, setting goals, and reaching them. Contests, too!

### THINKQUEST
http://www.thinkquest.org
Includes information on why and how to invest,
as well as on youth-friendly companies. Go to
http://library.thinkquest.org/3096/ for
ThinkQuest's stock market game.

### WALL STREET DIRECTORY
http://www.wsdinc.com
This Web site provides newsletters, sources for online trading, and
investment information.

## YOUNG BIZ.COM

http://www.youngbiz.com
Designed for young adults, this Web site has daily updates on Tommy
Hilfiger's, Disney's, and McDonald's stock. Check out its worldwide
stock market game—it awards great prizes.

The following Web sites offer online research:

## INVEST-O-RAMA

(www.wsdinc.com)

## INVESTORGUIDE

(www.investorguide.com)

## MONEY CENTRAL INVESTOR

(moneycentral.msn.com/investor)

## QUICKEN

(www.quicken.com)

## WALL STREET DIRECTORY

(http://www.wsdinc.com)

# Glossary

**AMEX (AMERICAN STOCK EXCHANGE):** Located in New York City, this exchange specializes in trading small- and medium-sized stocks.

**ANNUAL REPORT:** A summary of a company's business operations for the past year that includes profit, losses, income, and net worth.

**ASK PRICE:** The price specified by someone who wants to sell stock.

**ASSETS:** What is owned by a company or a person.

**BEAR MARKET:** A downward trend in the stock market.

**BID PRICE:** The price offered by someone who wants to buy stock.

**BLUE-CHIP STOCKS:** Stocks of large companies that have been in business for years and are financially strong.

**BONDS:** Loans made to the government and to corporations by investors, who receive a secure, fixed amount of interest.

**BROKER:** See *stockbroker*

**BULL MARKET:** An upward trend in the stock market.

**CAPITAL GAINS:** Profits from the sale of investments.

**CERTIFICATE OF DEPOSIT (CD):** Money lent to a bank for a specified period of time in exchange for a set rate of interest.

**COMMISSION:** A percentage of the buying or selling price of stock paid as a fee to a stockbroker.

**COMMON STOCK:** Stock issued by a corporation that gives you a part ownership in the company.

**COMPOUND INTEREST:** Interest paid on both the money you invested and the interest that has been added to it.

**CUSTODIAL ACCOUNT:** An investment account opened and managed by adults for minors until they reach maturity.

**DEEP DISCOUNT BROKER:** A low-cost brokerage that usually works through computers.

**DISCOUNT BROKER:**   A broker who charges a lower commission because the investor does all the stock research and tells the broker which stocks to buy or sell.

**DIVERSIFICATION:**   Putting money into a number of different investments.

**DIVIDEND:**   Payments to stockholders of their share of a company's profits.

**DOW JONES INDUSTRIAL AVERAGE:**   Information arrived at each day that tracks the performance of the stock market based on the average price of thirty blue-chip stocks.

**ELECTRONIC CERTIFICATE:**   Proof of purchase for stock on record in the computer files.

**FEDERAL DEPOSIT INSURANCE CORPORATION (FDIC):**   A branch of the federal government that insures the money placed in a checking or savings account, so you are protected if the bank fails.

**FEDERAL RESERVE:**   A branch of the U.S. federal government that sets interest rates in the United States.

**FINANCIAL PLANNER:**   Advises clients on all their financial dealings, helping to achieve their goals.

**FULL SERVICE BROKER/DEALER FIRM:**   A financial-services company that answers all your investing questions, gives advice, then buys or sells stock for you.

**GROWTH STOCKS:**   Stocks that pay little or no dividends because the investor's share of profits is reinvested into the company to help it grow.

**HIGH/LOW/LAST ON CLOSING:**   The highest, lowest, and last prices a stock was traded for during that day.

**INCOME:**   Money received from all sources.

**INCOME STOCKS:**   Common stocks that pay more in dividends and pay on a regular or quarterly basis, like income from a steady job.

**INCOME TAX:**   A percentage of a person's total income each year that is owed to the federal government.

**INDIVIDUAL RETIREMENT ACCOUNT (IRA):**   An investment account in which money is held for retirement with favorable tax treatment.

**INFLATION:**   Rise in the cost of living.

**INITIAL PUBLIC OFFER (IPO):**   The first offering of a company's stock to the public.

**INTEREST:** Money paid to you for the use of your money.

**INVESTMENT:** Putting your money to use in something that offers the possibility of good returns or profit.

**INVESTOR:** A person who chooses to risk money in buying and selling securities, hoping it will bring a profit.

**LARGE CAP (LARGE CAPITALIZATION) STOCKS:** The stock of companies that have over $5 billion in market capitalization.

**MARKET CAPITALIZATION:** The value of all a company's outstanding shares.

**MARKET-MAKER:** A specialist who works with trades of a particular stock.

**MARKET ORDER:** When the stockbroker is instructed to buy a certain stock at the best price set by the market maker.

**MATURITY DATE:** The agreed-upon time at which the money you paid for a bond must be returned to you.

**MUTUAL FUND:** A portfolio of stocks and/or bonds in which many people invest.

**NASDAQ (NATIONAL ASSOCIATION OF SECURITIES DEALERS AUTOMATIC QUOTATIONS):** This exchange began in 1972 and was formerly known for OTC (over-the-counter trading).

**NYSE (NEW YORK STOCK EXCHANGE):** This exchange began in 1972 in New York City. It is the largest stock exchange so it affects world trading.

**ONLINE TRADING:** Buying and selling stock via the Internet.

**PORTFOLIO:** The composite of all a person's financial investments.

**PORTFOLIO MANAGER (OF A MUTUAL FUND):** A person employed by the mutual fund who chooses what kinds of stocks and bonds to buy for the fund.

**PREFERRED STOCK:** Stock that gives investors an ownership in a company and set dividends, but no voting rights.

**PRICE/EARNINGS RATIO (P/E RATIO):** The price of a share of stock divided by the company's earnings per share.

**PROFIT:** The amount earned when a stock is sold for more than its price at purchase.

**RETURN:** Another term for profit; it may include interest or dividends.

**RISK:** Taking a chance.

**SHARE:** A percent of ownership in a company or corporation.

**SHAREHOLDER:** Someone who owns shares of a company stock (*stockholder*).

**SMALL CAP (SMALL CAPITALIZATION) STOCKS:** Stock of companies that have less than $5 billion in market capitalization.

**SPLIT:** Cutting the price of stock in half, giving shareholders twice as many shares, but each share worth half the former price.

**SPREAD:** The difference between the bid and ask price in the buying and selling of a stock.

**STOCK:** A share in a company.

**STOCKBROKER:** Someone who is hired to buy and sell stocks for investors (*broker*).

**STOCKHOLDER:** Someone who owns a share of company stock (*shareholder*).

**STOCK MARKET/STOCK EXCHANGE:** The business of buying and selling stock.

**TAX BRACKET:** Where your income places you according to the rates set by the Internal Revenue Service (IRS).

**TICKER SYMBOLS:** Shortened name or initials for each company listed on the stock exchanges.

**UNIFORM GIFT TO MINORS ACT:** A law that allows adults to give money to a minor to be held in the minor's name until she/he reaches maturity.

**UNITED STATES GOVERNMENT SECURITIES:** Treasury notes, bills, and bonds backed by the credit of the United States.

**VENTURE:** An undertaking involving risk or uncertainty.

**VOLATILE:** Sharp ups and downs in the stock market.

# Index